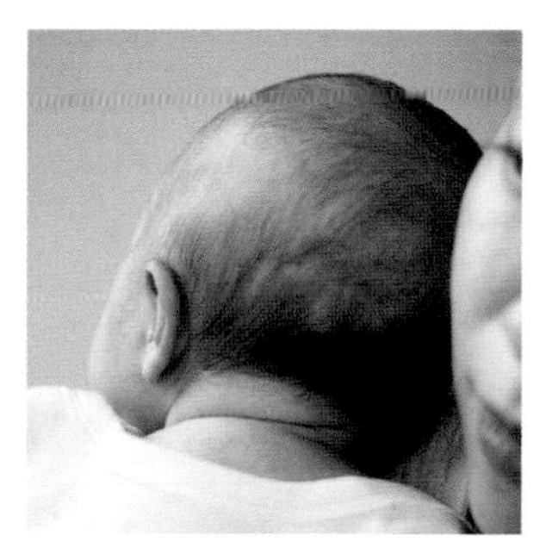

new mother's
survival guide

new mother's *survival guide*

RYLAND
PETERS
& SMALL
LONDON NEW YORK

CHERYL SABAN Ph.D.

senior designer Catherine Griffin
commissioning editor Annabel Morgan
picture researcher Emily Westlake
production Gemma Moules
art director Leslie Harrington
publishing director Alison Starling

First published in the UK in 2008
by Ryland Peters & Small
20–21 Jockey's Fields
London WC1R 4BW

First published in the United States in 2008
by Ryland Peters & Small
519 Broadway, Fifth Floor
New York, NY 10012

www.rylandpeters.com

10 9 8 7 6 5 4 3 2

ISBN 978-1-84597-713-9

A CIP record for this book is available from the British Library.

Printed and bound in China

contents

introduction

Motherhood has been described as both a blessing and a curse. There is no greater joy than holding our children close and gazing into their precious faces. Conversely, we can plumb the depths of despair if our children are in danger or hurting in any way.

As the mother of four, and the grandmother of four, I've experienced a wide spectrum of emotions with my children, and learned valuable lessons, which I'm happy to share. The initial stages of new motherhood, the gearing up for it, the challenges of the unknown, and the logistics of everyday life are both novel and delightful and, at the same time, intimidating. As you go boldly forth into this monumental new phase of your life, the ability to reach out to others for support, as well as a willingness to learn, will serve you well.

The *New Mother's Survival Guide* is not intended to take the place of medical reference books. There are many works of that sort available that more appropriately serve that purpose. However, I hope this little volume will be prove to be a welcome supplement and support to new mothers everywhere. The book provides a helpful overview of what to expect while you're pregnant, valuable practical information about pre-planning and home organization, and tips on how to navigate those first precious months of your child's life, and your first year as a mother... *Congratulations*!

plans and preparations

OK – it's official. You're going to be a mother! By now you've probably begun to feel some new bodily sensations, and your clothes might be getting a little tight. Along with the physical changes you're going through, of course you'll also be wondering what life will be like when your baby arrives. A life-altering shift occurs with the birth of a child. Things will never be quite the same again, but you can prepare for some changes in advance, and that may make you feel better equipped to deal with motherhood. New parents are often amazed by the sheer volume of new equipment and supplies they need, not to mention an entirely new list of personal contacts in your address book: doctors and birth coaches, baby stores and lactation specialists.

thinking ahead

nesting instinct

gearing up

Despite your feelings of excitement at being pregnant, gearing up for a new baby can feel overwhelming at times. Which of the hundreds of baby items on offer are really necessary? And when should one begin accumulating them? Beyond the logistics of setting up house, dozens of other questions will arise, too. What can I do to prepare for baby before the birth? How can I increase my own stamina for birth? And what happens immediately after delivery? The *New Mother's Survival Guide* will help you organize yourself ahead of time, so you can be just that little bit better prepared for life with baby!

different stages

Though the first few months of pregnancy may contain some queasy days or – even worse – bouts of morning sickness, most women feel energetic and glowing for the middle part – what's known as the middle trimester. At this stage, you'll most probably get the urge to nest – that instinctive desire to put your home in order in anticipation of the new addition to the family.

So before you reach the final countdown to your delivery date, when all you'll be able to think about is your baby's debut, take advantage of your mid-pregnancy energy burst to feather your nest, set up house, and revel in the sheer excitement of imminent motherhood!

pre-birth preparations

delivery choices

It's never too early to discuss delivery choices with your partner. Will you give birth in hospital, or are you considering a home birth? If a home birth is planned, quite a bit of forward planning is required – you may, for example, want to hire a pool for a water birth. Discuss your ideal delivery choices with your partner, your doctor and/or midwives, so you can work out a realistic birthing plan that is tailored to your needs.

your birth coach

Once you've decided on your preferred birth method, it's time to choose a birth coach. This could be your husband, your life partner, a relative, a friend, a doula (a trained labor support person) or even just your medical practitioner. Your birth coach should be informed about the birth process, so that he or she can encourage you through all the stages of your labor, while keeping a level head and calm approach.

new friends

An added benefit of parenting and pre-birth classes is the opportunity to meet and bond with other mothers-to-be. You may form new friendships with women in these classes that comprise part of your support group later. These relationships can also be the genesis of a future mother and baby group, so don't be shy – register to participate early.

the grand tour

Most hospitals offer prenatal instruction and parenting advice for parents-to-be, along with tours of the birthing rooms and the different facilities on offer – a birthing pool, for example. It's a good idea to sign up and take advantage of any such opportunities. Knowing what to do and where to go beforehand will boost your confidence and greatly reduce your anxiety when the time of birth arrives.

birthing and parenting classes

back to school...

Parenting classes are not only a great idea – they're extremely beneficial! Babies are not merely little adults; they're unique individuals, and a whole new set of skills must be learned in order to care for them. You and your partner will need to make adjustments to make room for a baby in your lives, and parenting classes will provide a strong foundation of knowledge for your upcoming new roles as parents. Learning a few parenting skills will reduce your anxiety, and help you build confidence in your new roles, too.

increase your stamina

Most pregnant women can continue with their usual exercise regime, although it's wise to check with your doctor about any strenuous exercise. Consider joining a prenatal yoga class. Yoga is great for relaxation, and classes also teach breathing exercises that can help while giving birth.

health and wellbeing

doctor, doctor

Your new baby will be a regular visitor to his or her doctor for well-baby check-ups, immunizations, developmental checks, and to address the occasional illness. Make sure you're signed up with a local surgery, or decide upon a pediatrician for your child before delivery. It's so important to have a health practitioner you trust and feel comfortable with.

in sickness and in health

It stands to reason that your prenatal health is vitally important for your unborn baby's health. Eat well, sleep plenty, and take gentle exercise. Regular check-ups for mothers-to-be should be part of your routine from the beginning of your pregnancy. And don't forget the dentist!

make a wish list

As a mother-to-be, you'll be eager to make decisions about how and when to set up your house for your new baby. In some cultures, friends and families throw baby showers or celebratory parties for expectant mothers, allowing well-wishers to give gifts before the birth. In other cultures, items for the baby are not even brought into the home until the baby is born. However, in both cases, mothers-to-be can get organized by selecting desired items for baby. Making lists of your preferred items will save you the time and effort of returning things that you don't need or want. Well before your delivery date, visit baby boutiques and department stores and acquaint yourself with all the available options. There are numerous brands and styles of car seats, strollers/pushchairs, highchairs, cribs/cots, bassinets/Moses baskets, rockers, swings, bedding, and baby clothes – the choices may seem endless! Many stores have a helpful list of the basic items that most new mothers will need, which makes the process that much easier. So take the opportunity – before baby arrives – to pick out your chosen items.

a
k

rock-a-bye baby

Of course you'll want to make space in your home for your new baby, and a little pre-planning will go a long way toward providing a smooth transition to life with the new arrival! Where will baby sleep? In a co-sleeper cot by your bed, or in a bassinet/Moses basket or cradle? Or will your baby go straight into his or her own room? Where do you plan to set up the all-important changing station? You may be surprised at the sheer number of diapers/nappies, baby wipes, and tiny T-shirts your baby gets through each and every day, so finding convenient storage space for all these items (and more) will help you slip into an easy routine when baby arrives.

spatial awareness

safety first

Though initially your baby will stay put in a small space, as soon as he or she is mobile you'll need to childproof your home – safety latches on kitchen cabinets, covers for all your electric sockets, and baby gates fitted on your staircases. Think ahead. For childproofing advice, look online or, if there's a store in your area that specializes in child-safety items, ask a consultant to come to your home to advise you on baby-proofing issues.

layette and baby basics

For those mothers who plan to set up their nursery before the birth, the planning and purchasing process can be spread out over several months. For those who choose to have layette and other items delivered after the birth, assign a family member or friend the task of calling the store with delivery details once the big day comes. Whatever your arrangements, you'll want your baby to come home to an environment that is clean, convenient, and comfortable and, most importantly, one that you feel comfortable in, too. The following lists should help you get started.

layette

Diapers/nappies: cloth or disposable.
Extra cloth diapers/muslins: for burp cloths and shoulder covers.
Wipes: several packages of chemical-free wet wipes.
Undershirts/vests: side-snap are easier at first, but the pull-over kind are good, too.
Kimono sets: tops and bottoms.
Receiving blankets: typically smaller and less bulky than normal blankets.
Booties/socks/hats
Ointment/cream: for diaper-/nappy-rash prevention.

basic baby supplies

Clothing: onezies/sleepsuits, undershirts/vests, socks, tops and bottoms, cardigans.
Bedding: fitted undersheets, mattress cover, unfitted sheets, soft, thin blankets for swaddling.
Furniture: bassinet/Moses basket, crib/cot, baby swing, baby recliner seat, stroller/pushchair, rocking chair (or other comfortable chair) for feeding, regulation newborn car seat.
Diaper/nappy bag: ready-stocked with travel-sized changing supplies for when you're out and about.
Baby-bop: (a V-shaped pillow that nestles round your waist to help support the baby during feeding).
Baby sling or wrap
Bottles, nipples/teats, sterilizer, bottle brush, pacifiers/dummies, breast pump, bottles for storing/ freezing breast milk.
Baby nail clippers and hairbrush
Infant milk formula: for those not breastfeeding. (And even if you are breastfeeding, it's good to have formula on hand in case of emergencies.)

new mother support network

As the saying goes, it takes a village to raise a child, which is why it's so important that new mothers get a support system of friends and family in place before baby arrives. Becoming a mother is not just one of many things you do – at first, it will seem like the *only* thing you do! Your usual activities will be forced to take a back seat to your main focus – your new baby. Even your partner may feel briefly sidelined as you spend every waking hour caring for a helpless, dependent-upon-you-for-everything infant. You may feel that your whole world revolves around your baby – and, to be honest, it will. Time for visiting girlfriends and partaking in other recreational activities may be scarce. But don't despair – balance will eventually return, and a new rhythm of life will evolve that includes you and your partner as a couple, you, your partner, and your child or children as a family and, lest we forget, it will even include you as an individual woman. In the meantime, get busy and build your support system!

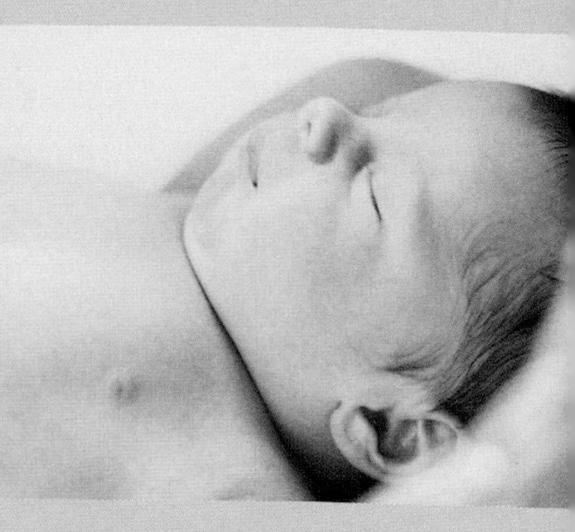

lines of communication

set up a phone tree

Set up a phone tree. Give one person the responsibility to be the first caller to dispatch information about you and your baby to a list of friends and family that you have prepared. Ring them once baby has arrived, and ask them to spread the good news!

create a family website

Some new parents create a special family website, so they can share first-glimpse photos and other pertinent information online. This is the fastest way to spread the news to friends and family. Don't forget to compile your email list in advance.

emergency phone list

Compile and print an emergency phone number list and post it by your house phone and in other prominent locations – such as the refrigerator or bulletin board. The list should include anyone you (or your support group) may need to contact in a hurry. Every individual involved in your medical team should be included.

Numbers to include:

Pediatrician
Midwife and/or doula
Local pharmacy
Your MD/GP's surgery and gynecologist/obstetrician
Your partner's office number and cell number
Your mother, father or other relative
Your partner's mother, father or other relative
Lactation specialist
Local market for delivery of groceries
Infant shop for delivery of pre-selected baby items
Good local restaurants – preferably ones that deliver!

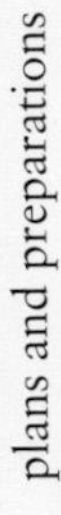

what lies ahead...

the best-laid plans

Being aware of the challenges you'll face is the first step toward overcoming them. The first week after birth can be unnerving, as so much has happened in such a short time, so your advance preparations should be geared toward making those early days calm and comfortable. Making a few simple plans so you can pre-empt any problems before they arise is a smart move. Everything about motherhood will be new – from the sleepless nights and complete devotion to your infant, to bleary-eyed mornings when you and your partner wonder what on earth happened to your life! A key theme is to reduce your stress levels whenever possible. For example, learning how to use your baby gadgets – the new battalion of sterilizers, wipe warmers, thermometers, and monitors – in advance will go a long way toward helping you stay calm and confident.

getting to grips with feeding

Even though breastfeeding is completely natural, and by far the best food source for your infant, be prepared for it to take a little getting used to – both for you and for your baby. If you do feel you need help, a lactation specialist will be a great comfort. You should be able to find one through your hospital or health visitor. Lactation specialists can explain what to do if your breasts become engorged or overly tender. She will also provide instruction and support if baby has a difficult time latching on, and will explain how to disengage your baby from your breast without discomfort. Don't forget to have a breast pump on hand, and work out how to use it before baby arrives. You don't want to find yourself poring over the instructions at a critical time.

gearing up for delivery

As the time draws near for your baby's birth, you'll be relieved you drew up your birth plan in advance. Once labor begins, the game is on. Whether you've chosen to have a home birth, or are planning to deliver in hospital, you need to be ready and prepared. Unless you've made an appointment to have an elective Caesarean section, it's impossible to predict the exact moment when your baby will arrive. Labor could start in the middle of the night; you could have a short, fast delivery, or struggle with it for hours, or even days. However it pans out for you, these will be thrilling moments. With your birth plan in place, you will be able to focus all your attention on your contractions and the birth, not the logistics.

lay in provisions

Prepare a shopping list of the foods you love, and include plenty of ingredients for easy-to-prepare meals. Place an order online, or ask a friend or family member to shop for you, so the refrigerator/fridge is full when you arrive home. It's one less thing for you or your spouse to worry about, and you will be grateful not to have to fuss over mealtimes. Include plenty of healthy snacks, fruits, vegetables, juices, and dairy products. And don't forget your supply of prenatal vitamins; your body will be working overtime, so you'll still need them!

cloth or disposable?

If you've decided to use cloth diapers/nappies, consider signing up with a diaper/nappy service, which will provide a delivery of freshly laundered cloth diapers/nappies and collect the soiled ones every week. If you plan to wash baby's diapers/nappies at home, lay in stocks of a laundry detergent that's gentle enough for baby's skin, and prepare to have the washing machine running morning and night! If you are going to use disposable diapers/nappies, ask for recommendations from other parents on the brands they like best.

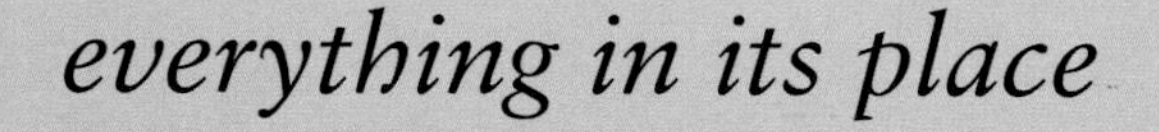

a comfortable chair

Move a comfortable chair – a rocking chair is nice – into your bedroom for breastfeeding or bottlefeeding baby. Place a small table or folding tray beside the chair to hold any extra items. You'll find that you'll always need space for a few extra bits and pieces – a cup of tea or glass of water, a burp cloth, maybe a radio, a clock, and the telephone.

making arrangements

older kids

If you have other kids who will need to be cared for, arrange with a relative or close friend to be on call for the big moment. If this requires overnight sleeping arrangements, set these up in advance as well. Tell the kids what plans you have made. Write out a schedule that gives explicit directions regarding bedtimes, meals, school. It's sensible to include emergency medical information, and a signed release form so that your pre-selected caregivers can obtain emergency medical treatment for your child or children if need be.

pet sitters

Arrange for pet sitters. Fish, birds, dogs and cats and other critters need to be fed and watered while you're away, too.

contact information

Have a cell phone with you, and all your contact information, just in case of emergencies.

advance plans

plan plenty of support

Of course your loved ones will want to help you during the earliest stages of new motherhood, and you'll value all their good intentions. But it's a good idea to think about some sort of helping and visiting schedule in advance, so that you aren't overwhelmed with help one day, then left alone to struggle on the next. Bear in mind that you will need time to recover from giving birth. Your body will have gone through enormous changes, and you may be exhausted. Don't be shy. Ask your family and friends for help, but on your terms.

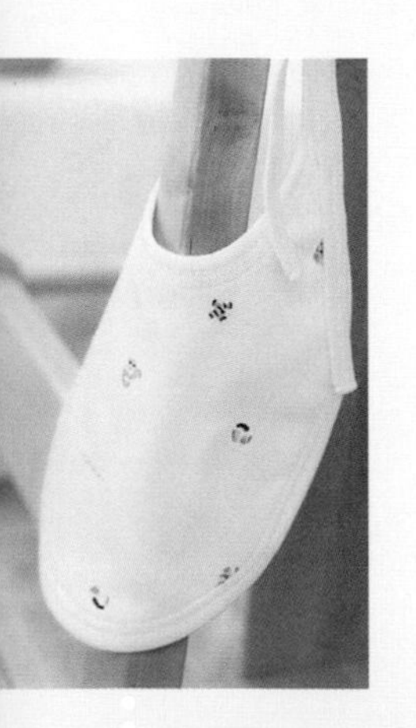

pack your bag

Pack a bag with a couple of days' worth of supplies and stow it near the door in case of a quick departure! In the excitement of labor, you may forget important or useful items.

Soft, comfortable nightgown with easy access for breastfeeding.
Socks (you may want these for labor)
One to three nursing bras.
Toiletries.
Underwear and a supply of heavy-duty menstrual pads/sanitary towels.
iPod, MP3, or personal CD player with soothing music.
Comfortable going-home clothes.
Going-home outfit for baby – a set that includes an undershirt/vest, onezie/sleepsuit, socks, hat, sweater, and soft, warm blanket.
List of important phone numbers for your partner to call!

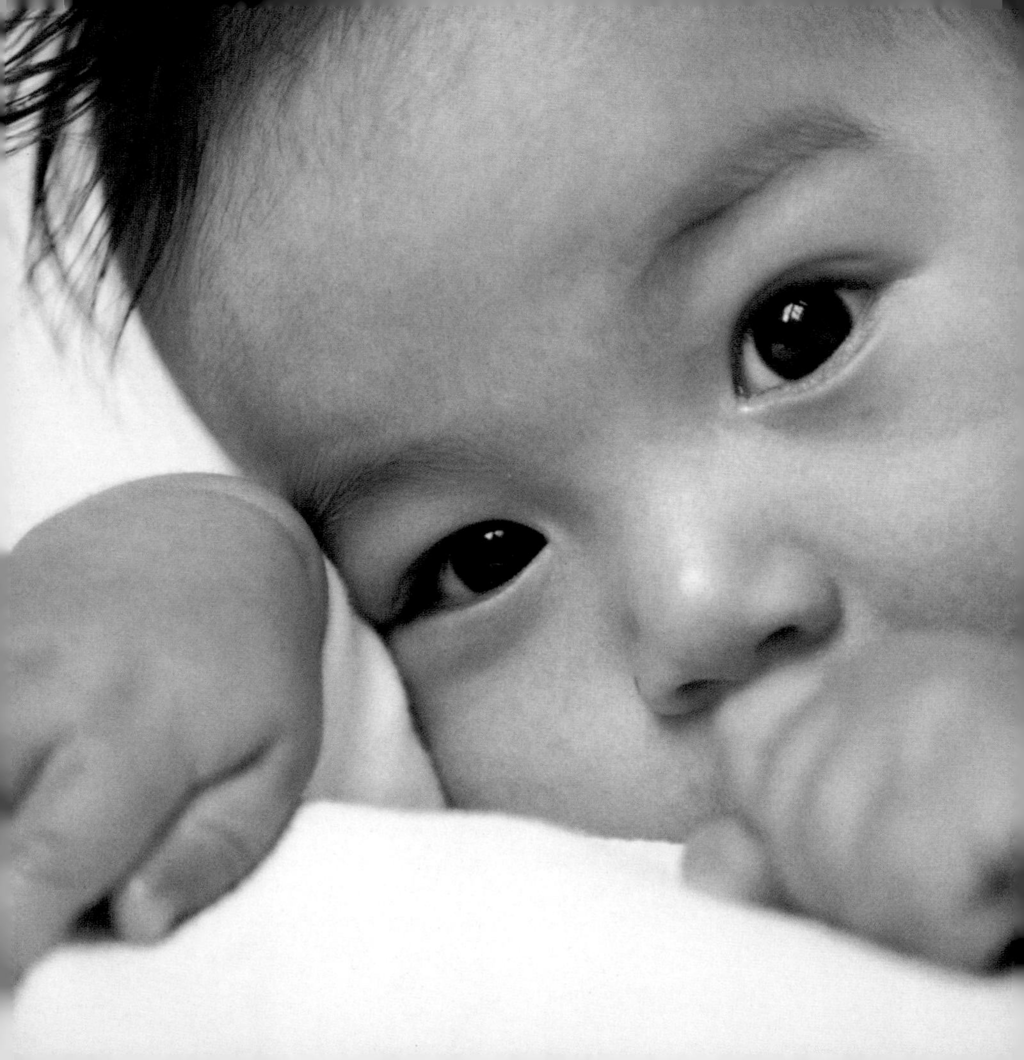

a new life begins

what to expect immediately after delivery

Now you've given birth, absolutely everything about your life will change. And, if this is your first baby, you'll probably have a lot of questions. What will the doctors do to your baby immediately after birth? How will you know when to breastfeed? If you have had stitches for an episiotomy, how long will it take to heal, and what can be done to reduce discomfort and pain? Regardless of whether this is your first child, or if this is a repeat performance for you, it's helpful to have some idea of what to expect immediately after delivery...

first moments

meeting your baby

Your first moments with your child will be exhilarating. It's a thrilling, earth-moving experience to hold and inspect your infant for the first time. You and your partner will be filled with emotion, and it is common for tears of happiness and relief to flow. After things calm down, your baby will be weighed and measured, and wrapped snugly in a blanket. Whenever baby is not in your arms, he or she should be wrapped in a blanket and/or placed in a warming bassinet to retain body heat.

breastfeeding

If you choose to breastfeed, your first feed will be a magical milestone; a moment you will long remember. Your baby will learn to suckle your breast when you offer it, though the process doesn't necessarily come naturally to everyone, so don't be surprised or despondent if it takes more than a few attempts before you both get the swing of it. Brushing your nipple across baby's cheek will trigger an instinct in your baby to turn its head towards your breast and "root," or seek the nipple. When you're in hospital, the midwives or nurses will be there to help you get baby latched on and feeding, and if you do encounter difficulties there will probably be a lactation specialist on hand to offer help and good advice. The realization that your body is producing everything your child needs to survive should not only make you feel powerful; it should also encourage you to take very good care of yourself!

early days

home time?

This depends upon you, your doctor, and the kind of birth you had. Many women go home after 24 hours or less. Others stay in hospital for a couple of days. If you've had a C-section, you'll stay in the hospital for several days. Even with a vaginal birth, if you can stay longer, the hospital provides a safe environment to recuperate, with help available while you adjust to motherhood.

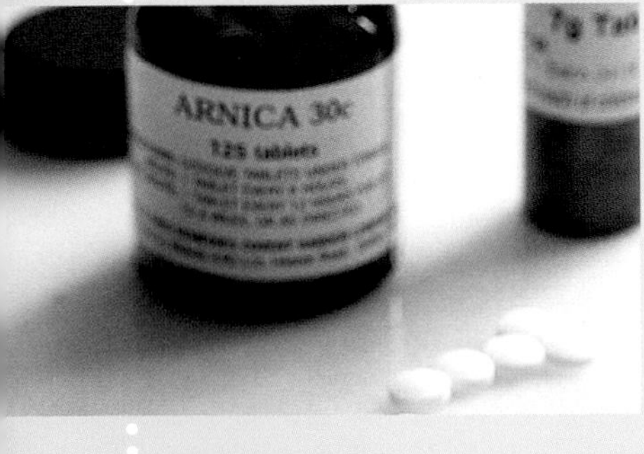

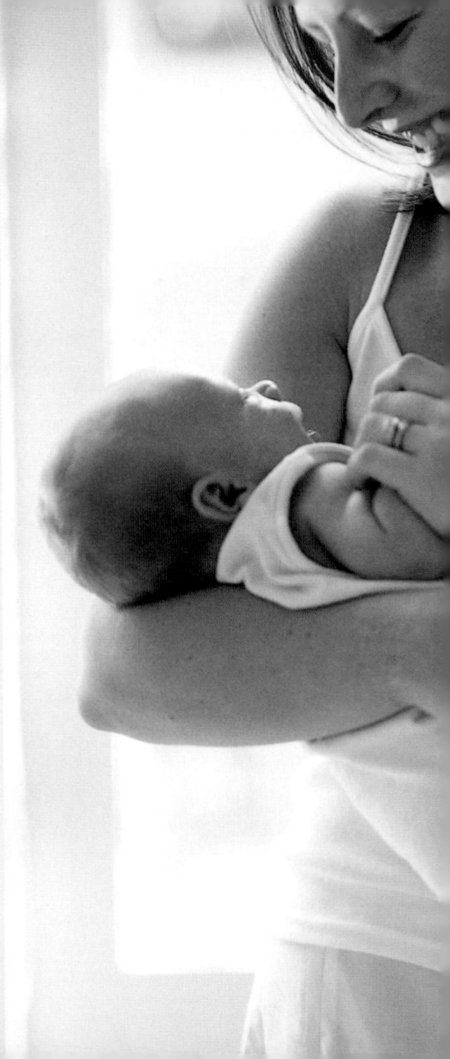

the first few days

Generally, most new mothers will have help from their partner and family and friends for the first couple of days after birth. Your main job during this time is to rest and regain your strength. Don't feel obliged to entertain dozens of guests, especially during those first few days after birth, and don't feel guilty about cutting visits short. It's normal to want some quiet time with your partner and new baby, and its essential that you get your rest. Ask your family and friends to take turns visiting, and spread out visitors so you can get the sleep you need. Besides, if you're breastfeeding, too much stress and excitement for you might translate to discomfort and tummy trouble for your baby. Though you'll want to share your excitement, the first few days are about recovery. Welcome your baby to the world with calm, and strive to surround yourself in tranquillity. After all, you all have some adjusting to do.

coming home

Bringing baby home from the hospital can be a nerve-racking experience. Bear in mind that you'll need to have a regulation infant seat fixed into your car, and baby must be secured in this seat, not your arms. You'll most probably sit buckled up beside your tiny bundle, while your partner takes the driver's seat. Be ready with a pacifier/dummy, if you choose to introduce one, or a clean finger for baby to suck on in case of a meltdown. If baby cries, you may work up a sweat, and your confidence may be momentarily compromised. Stay calm. If your baby gets very distressed, you can always pull over, stop the car, and breastfeed to calm baby down. Chances are, your infant will sleep peacefully through the journey, and you'll spend those moments adoringly gazing into your baby's beautiful face.

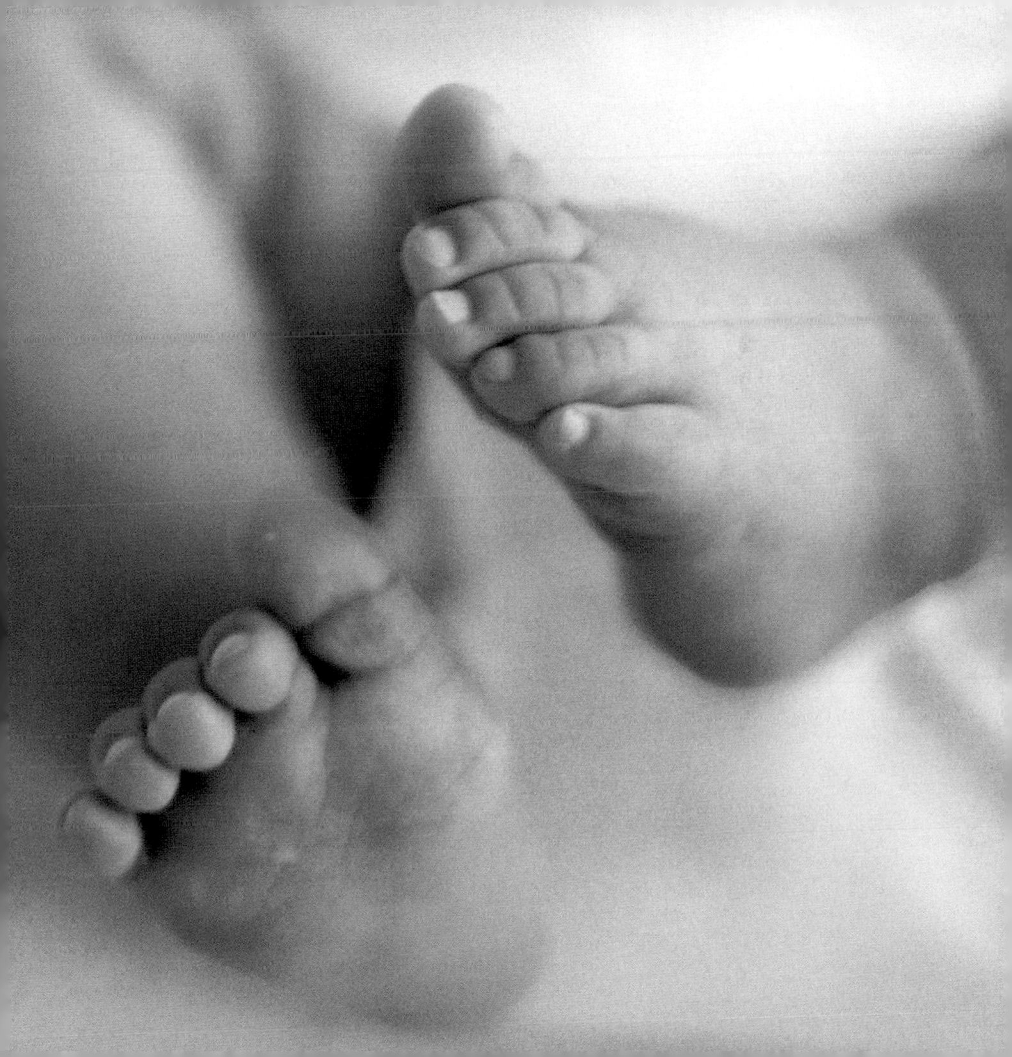

accepting help

For the first week, it's sensible to accept help whenever and however it is offered. One great way of allowing family to help and show how much they care is by asking them to help out with meals. After all, proper nourishment is vital for new mothers, especially if they're breastfeeding. The ideal breastfeeding diet includes lots of liquids, plenty of fresh fruit and vegetables, and sufficient protein at regular intervals, to give you the energy to cope with your new 24/7 schedule. When friends and family ask what they can do to help you, ask them to stock your freezer with home-made heathy meals that you only need to defrost and heat up.

taking care

on arrival

When you arrive home you'll want to settle into your bedroom, change the baby's diaper/nappy, then get into a comfortable position to feed your infant. At this critical moment, you'll be patting yourself on the back for organizing your feeding area in advance! Breastfeeding can be dehydrating, so you will probably want to have some water, juice, decaffeinated tea, or milk at hand.

looking after yourself

Not every birth requires an episiotomy (a small incision the doctor makes at the base of your vagina to avoid tearing) but if you had one, you'll also have stitches, and they can make the entire region feel tight and uncomfortable while they heal. While you're in hospital, you may be given ice packs and medication to help with any pain and swelling. Keep the area clean when you go home, and check with your doctor if your discomfort is extreme.

stocking up

important basics

If you already set up the basics before baby's arrival, the items you'll need during the first few days after birth will be ready and waiting for you at home. However, if you choose to wait until baby is born to bring in baby items, bear in mind that you won't have the time or energy to start washing baby clothes, bedding, and blankets as soon as you get home. Instead, ask a friend or family member to pre-wash all the baby bed linen, cloth diapers/nappies, baby layette, blankets, and any other items that will touch baby's skin, as well as to sterilize bottles, nipples/teats, and pacifiers/dummies. This is a good time for one of your new mother support team to step in and take charge!

stock the changing station

Ask your partner, friend, or family member to stock up the changing station, whether it be a traditional, purchased changing table, or a flat space on a bathroom counter. You need to have a wet-proof changing pad, diapers/nappies, organic or chemical-free baby wipes, undershirts, socks, plain cotton wipes and cotton swabs/buds all to hand.

feminine products

Don't forget to stock up your bathroom with the feminine products you'll need after birth, including menstrual pads/sanitary towels and nursing/breast pads.

washing up

Don't feel embarrassed about asking visitors to wash their hands before they handle the baby. Germs travel quickly via our hands. And it may sound overly protective, but it's best not to let small children touch baby's hands or face at all in the very beginning.

house rules

Many new mothers prefer to keep visitors to a minimum in the first couple of weeks, to allow everyone in the new family to adjust, and to reduce the chance that visitors may unwittingly expose you or baby to an illness. Trying to be a hostess requires energy that may be in short supply, so save it for the important things – like baby, yourself, and your partner. You have the right to decide when and how many guests you'll allow at one time, so be firm if it all feels like it's getting out of hand.

visiting hours

baby needs

New babies have a lot of needs, and they'll be depending on you to meet them all. They need to have their diapers/nappies changed eight to ten times or more a day. They need to be kept cozy, snug, and dry. They need to be fed on demand in the beginning, but certainly no less than every couple of hours. They need to be cuddled, they usually like to be rocked, and they need to sleep. Though babies can sleep up to 16 hours a day, their sleeping schedule is likely to be erratic and won't necessarily coincide with your sleeping routine. New mothers will soon find that, if they are to get the sleep they crave, they must adjust to baby's timetable at first, and this can be tricky, since newborns rarely (if ever!) follow an exact schedule.

when baby cries...

When your baby cries, she or he is using an instinctive tool to alert you. For the time being, it is the only method of communication they have. Before you panic and assume something is wrong, check the basics: Is your baby wet? If so, it's time for a clean, dry diaper/nappy. Babies don't necessarily enjoy being changed, so be prepared for a bit of fussing. But, generally, once your infant has been cleaned, changed, and held close to you, he or she should calm down. If your baby cries inconsolably, **call your doctor** for advice. There may be something that needs to be addressed.

temperature

Though you may want to wrap up your infant in an effort to comfort him or her, the blanket you use should be relatively lightweight. Pay attention to your baby's temperature. He or she won't be comfortable if it is too hot, or too cold.

hunger

When was the time of baby's last feed? How many minutes did your baby nurse? In the first few weeks after birth, most babies should be fed on demand. You may want to keep a notebook near your nursing chair so you can keep track of how many minutes baby breastfeeds and remember which side baby fed from, or how much formula your baby has consumed.

if in doubt...

When in doubt about baby's welfare, **call your doctor**. Pediatricians/GPs are accustomed to anxious new mothers, and will be ready and willing to answer your questions or allay any fears. Don't ever be embarrassed to seek professional advice.

what can I do?

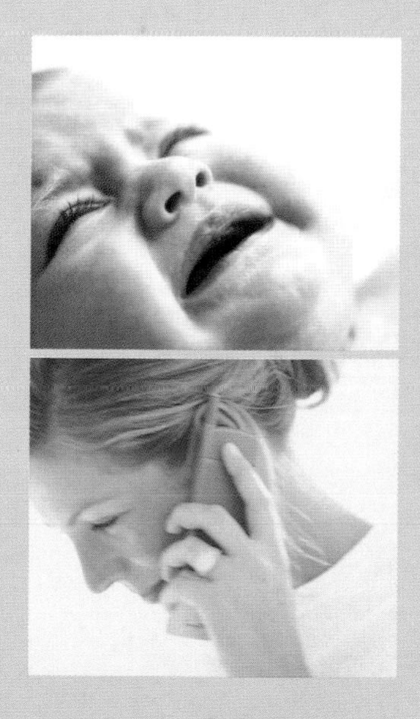

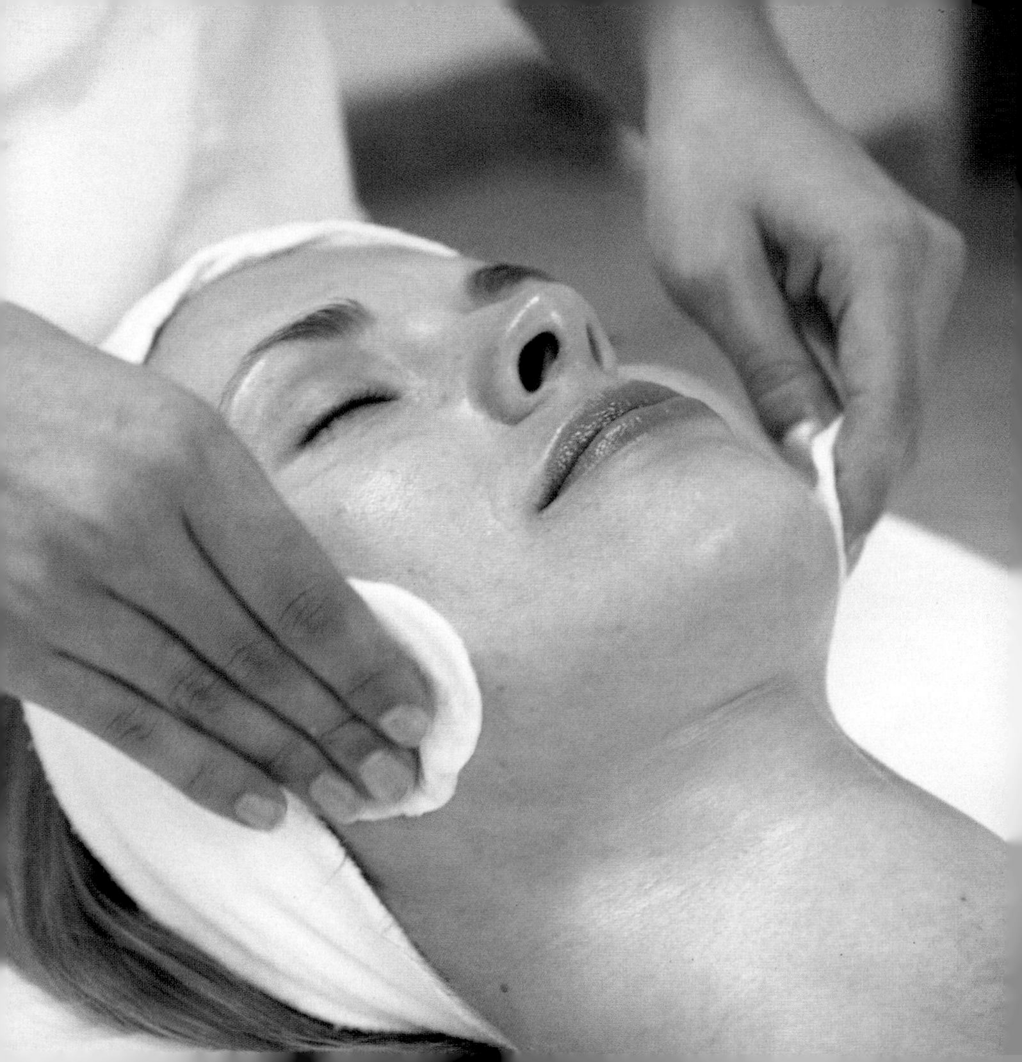

your needs

New mothers have a lot of needs, too, and the first week or so of your new life may seem overwhelming. Recovering from birth requires rest, a calm environment, and good nutrition. You will be functioning on less sleep than you're used to, and post-pregnancy hormones may be wreaking havoc with your emotions. If you have difficulty soothing your baby, you may feel inadequate, or at a loss as to what to do. It's only normal to experience some ups and downs as you adjust to your status as a mother, but try to keep a sense of perspective, and remember that the difficult times will pass. It doesn't take long before you become an authority on all things regarding your own child. In the meantime, however, be prepared to reach out for help if you need it.

ups and downs

call upon your new parent posse

If you met other moms-to-be during your pregnancy, now is the time to pick up the phone to them. Sharing ups and downs, lessons learned, and funny stories, as well as difficulties, with someone who understands, can feel like you've been tossed a life-ring in a stormy sea. Friendships with other new mothers can reinforce your confidence in yourself, and allows you to voice your feelings to those who can truly relate to them, because they're in the same boat.

the baby blues

The whole process of gearing up for a birth, the nine months of waiting and wondering, and the excitement of holding your newborn for the first time can be overwhelming at a time when your hormones are already making you emotionally fragile. The baby blues isn't a hollow phrase – it's a real issue that many new mothers face. Post partum blues and post partum depression can occur as a result of the radical hormone changes that occur during and after birth. The blues can also be exacerbated by a difficult birth, a lack of sleep or a fussy, crying baby. Help from friends and family and getting enough rest are important antidotes. But if your baby blues become severe, and you can't seem to shake them, see your doctor ASAP. Don't hold back – if you sense that your mood is dark, and sadness or apathy is taking over, reach out immediately for help. You are not alone – many mothers find their post partum a trying experience, but there are therapies and medications that can help you get over this hump.

problem solving

rough delivery

If you had a rough delivery, your healing time could be longer than is usually expected, requiring patience and strength that may be in short supply. Trying to recover, cope with pain, bond with your baby, connect with your partner, and regain some semblance of normality in your life can seem like daunting tasks. This is the time to lean on your new mother support group to make sure you don't overdo it. Reach out to your doctor or midwife, a psychological therapist, or, if the spirit moves you, your spiritual or religious counselor for regular chats. Communication is key – share your feelings, and allow others to help. Enlisting the aid of a doula or maternity nurse can help. The efforts of a trained compassionate helpmate may help alleviate stress and the subsequent negative impact that high levels of stress hormones can have on you during this time.

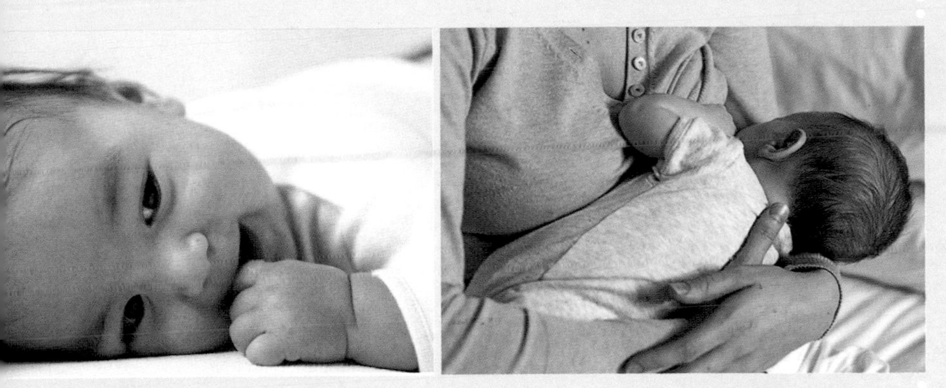

breastfeeding

The frustrations of the breastfeeding learning curve can cause new mothers to become stressed. Breasts and nipples can become tender and sore and the prickly sensation of the "milk drop" or "let down" can take some getting used to. Some babies do find it difficult to latch on to the breast properly, and therefore are not getting the nourishment they crave, as well as making it painful for their mother. Breastfeeding moms may need a lactation specialist to promote a comfortable nursing experience.

getting help

Obtain the name of a psychologist or family therapy specialist and keep it handy, in case you become overwhelmed with your new challenges as a mother.

do not disturb

With a newborn, sleep is vital, though it may be fleeting and sporadic. A good rule is to try to take catnaps while your baby sleeps. Resist the urge to tidy closets or return emails – lie down and rest! Even if you can't sleep while baby is sleeping, deep-breathing exercises or relaxing meditation will be restorative. It's all about regaining strength. Your new responsibilities as a mother require you to be in condition to run the marathon of your life. Your baby will wake and want to nurse every couple of hours, and most probably more often than that, so sleep is a valued commodity. Grab all the sleep you can, and guard your quiet time judiciously.

relax...

Enlist someone to give you a shoulder, neck or foot massage. You'll be so focused on your new baby that your own welfare may get short shrift. A cup of decaffeinated tea or other soothing drink and a shoulder massage can help you stop, sit down, relax, and focus on yourself for a moment.

a hand to hold

New mothers need understanding, cuddling, and a warm hand to hold – especially after several sleep-deprived nights pacing the floor with a crying baby. Your partner's hugs and cuddles will mean a lot to you during this time, especially because your roles as part of a couple have changed, and you must now adapt to life as a threesome (or more, if you already have children). Though sex is not advisable immediately after birth, hugs, kissing, and intimate private time is essential.

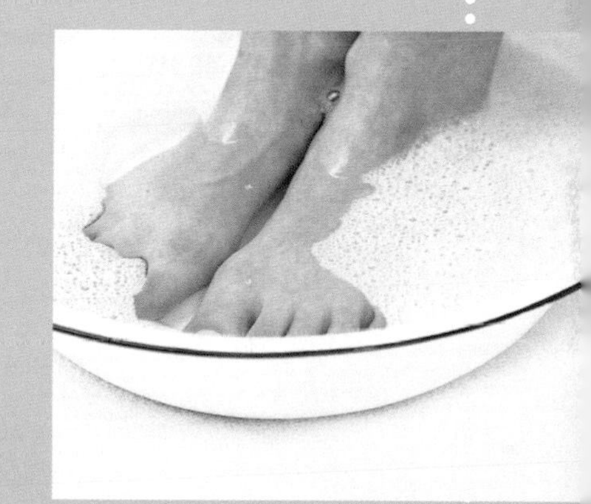

gaining support and strength

new grandparents

Your parents and in-laws have suddenly taken on the new role of grandparents. It's a thrilling time, when mothers and fathers watch their sons and daughters become mothers and fathers. But even this happy new development in the family tree can involve growing pains. Remember that a new family role has been added, and therefore the dynamics of your relationship with your parents may change. New grandparents may want to be more involved in your life now that a grandchild has appeared, or alternatively they may not live near you and may therefore be unable to participate in your child's life as much as they or you would like. There may even be jealousy between in-laws, if one set has more access to the new baby than the other. Try not to be drawn into any family dramas. Keep things in perspective. Though your parents and in-laws are an extension of your family, it is OK for you to set the boundaries in your own home.

You may receive lots of advice from your parents. Some of it you'll agree with, while the rest may not fit into your conception of parenthood. Set the tone from the beginning, so you can encourage your family members to work together. You can avoid hurt feelings and resentments by gently and lovingly communicating your boundary wishes, while remaining open to your parents' proffered advice. Make an effort to participate in ongoing family rituals, and encourage both sets of grandparents to be part of your baby's life. The goal is to ensure that your baby is surrounded by the most important gift your family can give – their unconditional love.

new you

Your body may not bounce back into shape in the first few days after birth, and that shouldn't surprise you. Though physical changes have been part of your life for the past nine months, now that your baby has been born, and you've shed the most important part of your baby weight, you may be impatient for the extra layer of padding to disappear as well. Give yourself a break. You are already on an emotional rollercoaster, so there's no need to add more stress to the ride. Just keep reminding yourself that regaining your shape *is* within the realm of possibility, even if it doesn't feel like it right now!

Breastfeeding is one way to help your body regain its pre-baby shape because it aids uterine contractions, helping your tummy muscles regain their strength. Walking is the perfect exercise. Try to eat a balanced diet at regular intervals, comprised of hearty wholegrains, fresh fruits and vegetables, and protein, to keep your energy supplies up and your sugar levels constant. As your strength slowly returns, you'll be able to start a more robust exercise routine. But in the meantime, take gentle walks around the block with your baby, enjoy the fresh air, and eat healthy meals. Believe it or not, with these basic, commonsense steps, you'll soon begin to see your body regain its former shape.

New fathers have a lot of new responsibilities when baby arrives. In his own way, he'll be exhausted from the birth experience, too. He most probably has been at your side throughout, and present at the birth of your child as well. We tend to take the birth of babies for granted, but it is a miracle every single time it works, and your partner has just witnessed an incredibly emotional and physically challenging event. His life, just like yours, has been irrevocably changed with the arrival of your child.

There is a danger that new dads can feel left out or underappreciated when baby arrives especially if you are breastfeeding, for he may feel shut out of, and unable to participate in, the feeding/bonding ritual. Remember that new dads have been riding their own emotional rollercoaster, and they also need time to adjust. He may feel that he's having to compete with the baby for your attention, which in the beginning may be true. You are both developing new roles, so keeping the lines of communication open is essential. Share your thoughts and feelings with your partner, and take time to listen to his in return. Whenever possible, share responsibilities for the care of your baby with your partner. He'll relish some private bonding time with baby, and you will benefit from his help and participation.

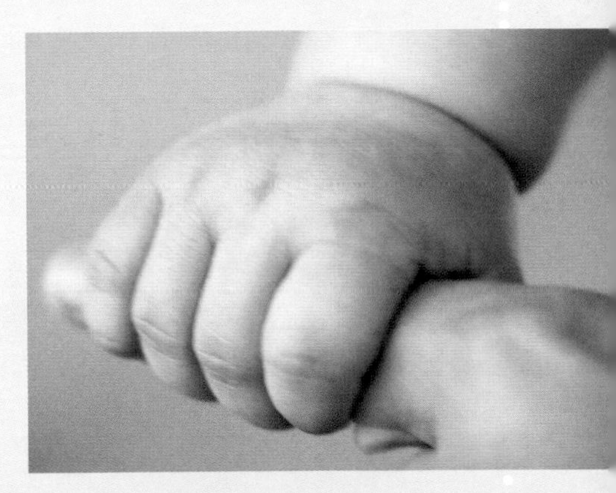

daddy needs

getting involved

daddy time

It's a good idea to create an informal job-sharing program that allows the new daddy to get involved. Dads can handle bathtime and diaper-/nappy-changing duties, and strolling, cuddling, and rocking baby too. They can also help with feeding time if you are bottle-feeding. And even if you're breastfeeding, once your supply is established, after two or three weeks you can express breast milk for bottle feeds between nursing times, so Dad can enjoy this special bonding experience and you can have a break.

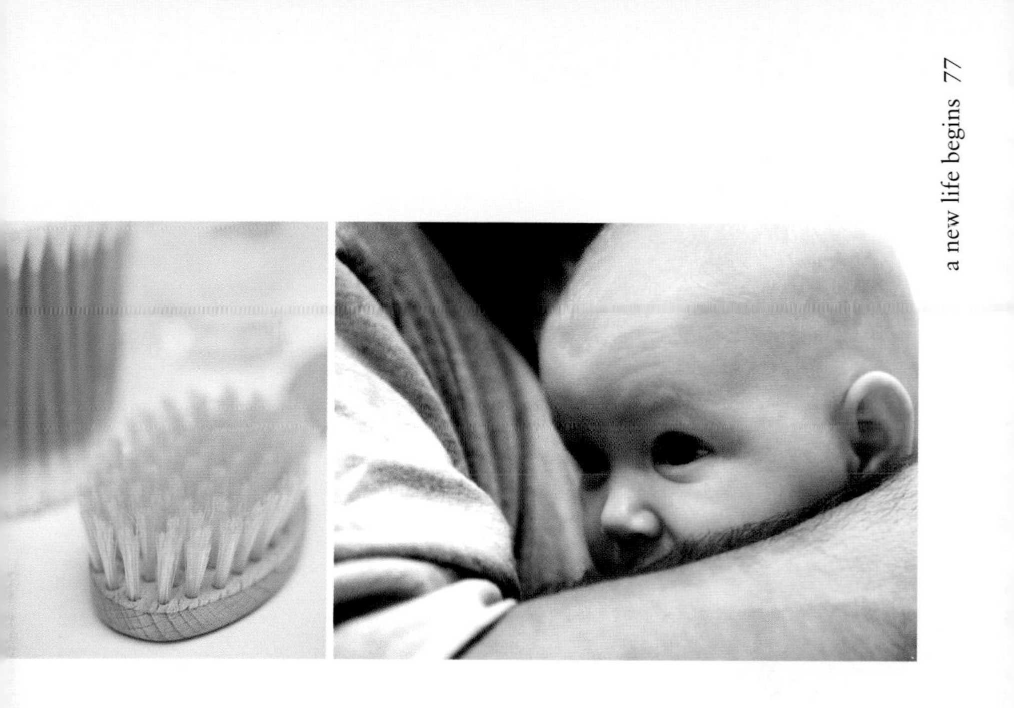

learning curve

New dads have a pretty steep learning curve of their own to deal with. The new dynamic of fatherhood can take some getting used to. Remember that you are both on the same side, and your goal is to raise a happy, healthy child together.

father/child outings

Prepare a Dad-specific, more masculine backpack diaper/nappy bag for the new dad to use on daddy and baby outings. He'll appreciate having a kit of his own!

show your appreciation

No matter how tired you are, try to acknowledge your partner's efforts. A smile of appreciation or thanks and a hug from you will go a long way.

energy boost

New dads need to take breaks, too. Often, the simple pleasure of engaging in a sport or hobby can raise the spirits of a weary new dad and replenish his energy reserves.

build a support group

Don't forget that new dads will need a support group of their very own. Your partner's perspective on family life might be entirely different than yours, and you may find that he handles his confusion, frustration, or tiredness in different ways, as well. Encourage your partner to make friends with other new dads and, if possible, to hang out with peers who are also parents.

working together

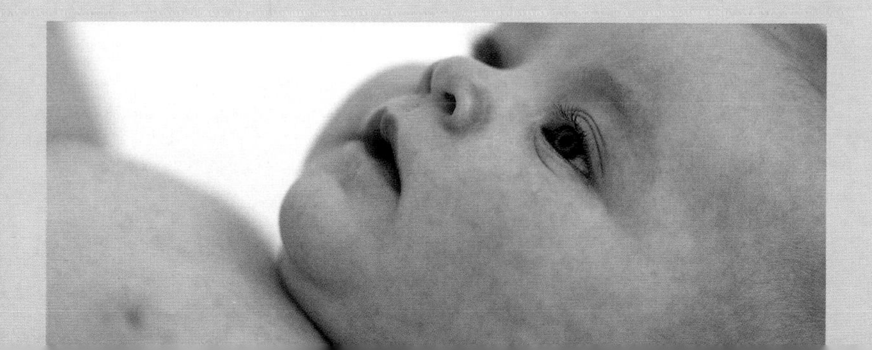

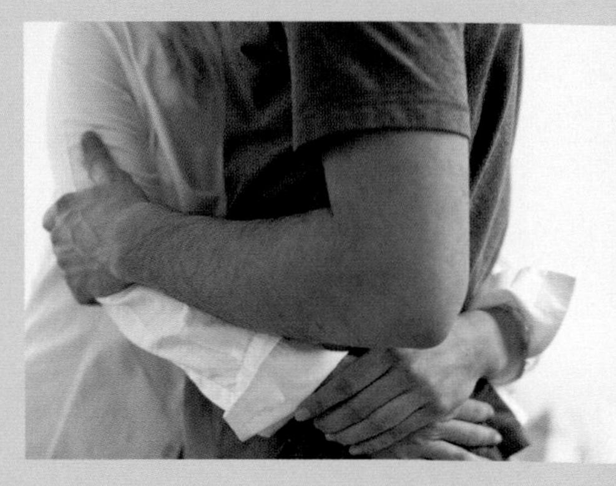

couple needs

In the middle of all the change and adaptation that a new baby demands, you and your partner need to find some time for each other. Your roles have both changed dramatically, and your responsibilities, time constraints, sleeping schedules, career priorities – basically, your entire lives! – are radically different now. You may be concerned about how soon to resume your sex life, and worried that you don't have the strength or motivation for sexual intimacy at first, either. Just take it slow – and try not to put too much pressure on each other. Bear in mind that intimacy and private couple time is important, however, and although such interludes needn't necessarily always lead to sex you'll want to resume that most intimate part of your relationship as soon as it's medically allowed, so you can keep the bond between you strong.

growing as a couple

Learning to be selfless, which is an essential new parent tool, doesn't mean that you must forego your sense of self, or disregard your relationship as a couple. In fact, the opposite is true. Your self-nourishment, as well as your continued enrichment and growth as a couple, is as important as ever. Though time is in short supply, take any spare moment to acknowledge that you love and miss each other. Admit that you would love to have uninterrupted conversations, romantic dinners, and intimate moments together, and make a date to do so. Making a concerted effort to regain your pre-birth connection as a couple will dispel any lurking fears or disappointments about the way life has changed, and will put a dampener on rising tension. If you're aware from the start of your newly minted parent status that couple time will be stretched, you can find new ways to not only be a new mother and father, but also the man and woman that started on this path to begin with.

emotional balance

one-on-one time

Ask a trusted family member or friend to visit regularly to hold/rock/cuddle your baby, so that you and your partner can enjoy some private one-on-one time. This is a great opportunity for new grandparents to lend a hand and feel involved. Go on a date, even if your rendezvous can only be a quick dinner at a local restaurant. At the very least, carve out some uninterrupted time to share a cup of tea.

a good, long hug

Check in with each other emotionally. Take a shower together, hold hands, give each other a hug. You may be surprised to learn that a good, long hug (20 seconds or more) releases feel-good chemicals in our brains. So hug often, and allow your happiness meter to be recharged!

communicate honestly

Make time to talk together as a couple, even if only for a few moments at a time. Discuss aspects of your life other than the baby, to remind yourselves of the world outside; you may have become so focused on your baby that you have neglected to notice the bigger picture. Ask a family member or trusted friend to watch baby for a short time – even just 10 minutes – so you can walk around the block hand in hand, just the two of you. Share your concerns, your problems, your fears, and your dreams. Remember that parenthood is a new experience for both of you. Try not to be overly territorial about it – share the joy of it, instead.

sharing the load

financial responsibilities

As a couple, you may feel pressured by all the new financial responsibilities inherent in parenthood. It's not uncommon for new mothers to feel conflicted about how they'll balance motherhood with their careers. Work out a budget together, and discuss your immediate anxieties, as well as any long-term worries. By laying the facts out in the open, you'll have a better sense of what you can do together to make the best of your circumstances, whatever they may be.

Breastfeeding and bottle-feeding are the two main choices available to provide nourishment for your new baby. While you'll find that both options have their pros and cons, breastfeeding is generally considered to be the optimum choice, simply because breast milk is entirely natural, always available, always at the right temperature, and perfectly provides for all your baby's nutritional needs. However, there may be circumstances that prevent you from breastfeeding, such as illness, or other unforeseen problems. And some mothers just find it too difficult to get to grips with breastfeeding, despite their best efforts. Bottle-feeding with a prepared baby formula would then be your feeding option, and you can rest assured that a well-balanced baby formula will provide for your baby's nourishment needs just fine.

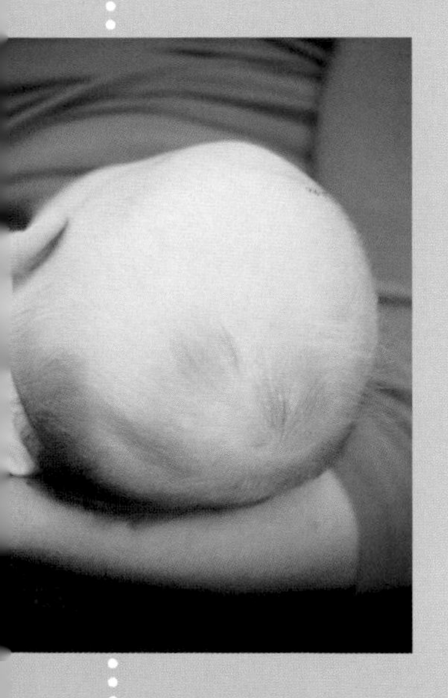

Whether you breast- or bottle-feed, you'll probably make a choice about your feeding preference before your baby is born. A discussion with your pediatrician/midwife prior to birth can help to shine a light on the issue for you, and help you make the choice, hopefully without pressure or guilt, that is right for you *and* your baby.

feeding your baby

breastfeeding

Breast milk actually adapts its composition to suit the needs of your baby. In the first few days, it provides the protein-rich colostrum your baby needs, and then changes into the higher-fat-content, more liquid version of mature breast milk. Breast milk offers additional health benefits to baby, and is available on tap – as long as you are around!

getting to grips with breastfeeding

Just because the creation of milk is a naturally occurring bodily function for new mothers, this doesn't mean the act of breastfeeding is particularly easy, effortless, or painless. Some new moms find it difficult to get the hang of breastfeeding, and may become frustrated and defeated. Sometimes babies don't latch on properly, and often the nipple and surrounding areola become tender and chapped. New mothers need to call upon their support system to back them up at these crucial times. It's important to ask for help rather than to struggle on alone, because the stress of breastfeeding complications can quickly make new mothers feel disheartened, and can exacerbate the problem. Lactation specialists are experts in breastfeeding, and are especially useful in difficult circumstances. These knowledgeable, compassionate specialists can help new mothers devise a nursing schedule for multiple births, as well.

modesty and inhibitions

When you're out and about, you may find that you need to breastfeed in a public place. If you feel uncomfortable or awkward about breastfeeding in front of other people, plan in advance for ways to protect your privacy. One rule of thumb is to choose your clothing carefully. Some loose blouses and tops offer easy access for the baby, while still providing enough coverage for you. A good solution is to carry a lightweight blanket with you that you can toss over your shoulder. It will provide a tent of coverage behind which your baby can nurse peacefully out of view.

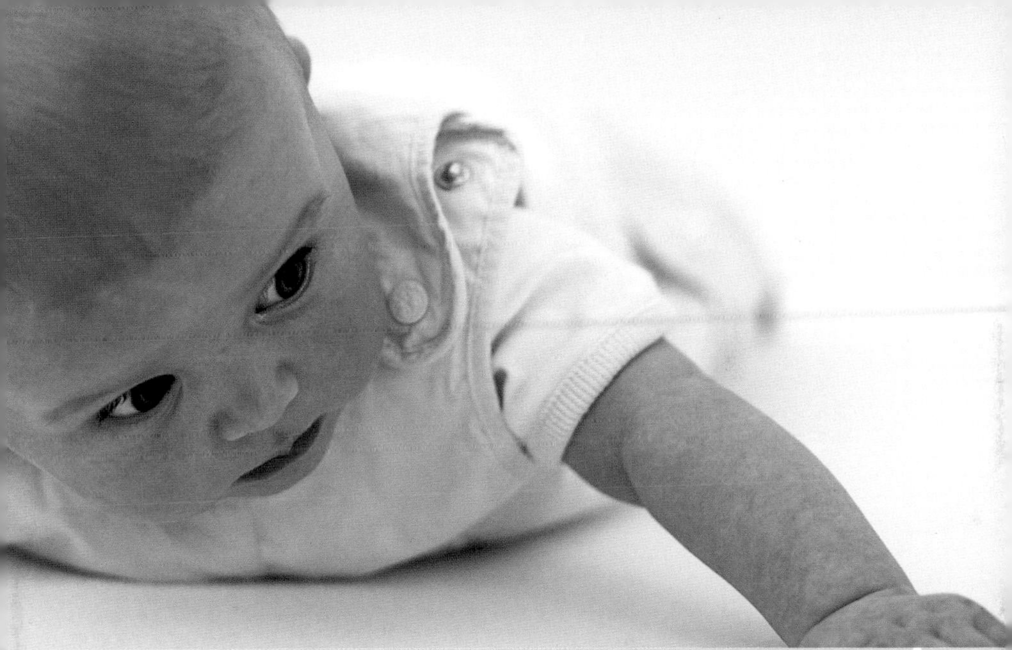

working girl

Some new mothers have to return to work sooner than others, and they have no choice but to augment their breastfeeding with bottle-feeding. This is when breast pumps really come in handy. Both manual and electric models are available, allowing you to express your breast milk in advance, and store it in special bottles (in the fridge or freezer) for those feeds when you cannot be present. As long as you keep up the pumping and nursing routine, your breasts will continue to produce milk, so don't automatically assume you'll have to drop breastfeeding when you go back to work.

bottle-feeding

The beauty of bottle-feeding is that it gives both parents a chance to participate in this important part of baby's care. Feeding times can be quiet, soothing, and bonding experiences. New mothers and fathers can take it in turns to feed baby, and give each other some well-deserved time off in between.

stock up

Keep an adequate supply of formula on hand. There are several types of formula available, including powdered formula and a ready-to-feed bottled variety. Choose whichever will be most convenient for you.

take care

Take care when you heat up baby's bottle. The milk should *not* be hot – lukewarm is preferable, but room temperature is fine too. *Always* test the temperature of your baby's formula before you feed him or her.

back to work

When new mothers have to return to work outside the home soon after giving birth, bottle-feeding will help ease that separation. Your baby will soon grow accustomed to happily accepting his or her bottle of milk from caregivers other than you.

the magic formula

Modern-day baby formulas have come close to duplicating the composition of mother's milk and, while baby formula won't adapt to your baby's needs exactly as breastmilk can, your baby will grow and thrive on formula just fine.

sleeping

Some babies settle into a regular and fairly predictable sleeping/ waking schedule after a few weeks. Others (unfortunately!) take months to find their circadian rhythm. If possible, it's best not to get too hung up on perfect schedules in the first couple of months, because baby's snooze time can be utterly unpredictable, and frustratingly random. All in all, newborns generally sleep 15 to 16 hours per day.

good sleep habits

After a couple of months, you may want to establish a routine or some daily rituals to follow to help your baby associate certain activities or events with naps and bedtime. There are many techniques for helping a baby soothe itself to sleep at the correct times. Some helpful tips to begin the process include:

Sleepy-time music: set up a CD player and play soothing sleepy-time music.

Pull the shades and turn off the lights: babies seem to sleep better in a cool, darkened room, away from the hustle and bustle of daily household activity.

White noise: run a fan, humidifier, air filter, or other "white noise" maker to help mask abrupt outside sounds. A CD that plays the pulsing sounds of a uterus appeals to some babies and might be a good idea in the first few weeks.

Wrap your baby snugly: some moms swaddle their babies – an ancient technique that keeps babies from startling themselves with their involuntary movements. Swaddling babies can make them feel more secure, and may remind them of the tight quarters they occupied in your womb! Discontinue swaddling before three months, as at that point the constriction may annoy your baby.

Resist rocking: though it is comforting to rock your baby to sleep, try to resist making this into a habit. You'll regret it when you have a bouncing (and hefty) ten-month-old who requires 30 minutes of rocking to get off to sleep! Instead, rock your baby just until it is drowsy and ready for sleep. Then gently put them down (on their back), to fall asleep alone. Your baby will soon become used to the feeling of falling asleep in its own bed, rather than in your arms.

back to normal

After a few weeks, your life will slowly begin to take on more of a predictable rhythm. Your baby may or may not be sleeping through the night (most likely not!), but you'll be surer of yourself, more confident, and more able to snap back into your old routines. And, hopefully, you'll have figured out a way to catch up on your sleep. Some new mothers will have several months of maternity leave, while others resume outside work much sooner. If you have a career that requires you to work outside the home as well as inside, it will soon be time to get back to it, and also to take up some of your other pre-baby activities. Hobbies, book clubs, exercise, evening classes – bring them all back on board, so you can establish a new rhythm of life as a mother.

setting goals

back up to speed

If you have begun to feel a little stir-crazy at home with baby all day, now's the time to get out and about and more actively involved in the world around you. If you have been on maternity leave, get ready to go back to work. Other ideas include:

Schedule family fun time If you have other children in the home, spend private time with them so they don't feel too left out by the new sibling. Take occasional excursions with the entire family, too – baby included.

If you're a work-at-home mom, add more adult stimulation by taking a class, learning a new skill, or starting a new hobby.

exercise routines

Fitting exercise into your life is not only important, it's crucial to your overall wellbeing. You can begin to exercise as soon as your doctor tells you it is safe. By now you should have gotten used to enjoying the fresh air by pushing your infant around the block, but after a couple of weeks, or when you get the go-ahead from your doctor, you'll be ready to take on more strenuous exercise.

be sociable

Being at home alone with a small baby can feel lonely, so join a mother and baby group, or set up informal weekly visits with other new mothers, so you can share advice, discuss concerns, and make new friends. Many new mothers find that their new parent posse grows into a close network of friends that they rely on for many years to come.

out and about

Meet friends and family for shopping and casual lunches in places where strollers/pushchairs and infants are welcomed, and where you feel you fit in nicely. Babies may cry or fuss, and require a diaper/nappy change during these outings, so seek out environments that are baby-friendly. Give yourself plenty of time to get going – each excursion takes lots of preparation. Loading and unloading all baby's equipment will take extra time, space and effort. Diaper/nappy bags, baby slings and strollers/pushchairs are now your constant companions!

the dating game

Set up a regular "adult" date night for you and your partner. Dressing up, putting on make-up, and leaving the house can be exhilarating – especially after feeling housebound for weeks. Ask a family member or friend to watch your baby for an hour or two, and then go out, look sexy, and enjoy being a woman again!

a normal rhythm

important practicalities

your newborn's health: know the warning signs for illness

Though we are loath to think of it, babies sometimes get sick. As a new mother, it's important to be prepared, and only sensible to know some of the danger signs. If your baby has any of the following symptoms, it could be a sign that he or she is ill and needs to visit the doctor immediately:

- **Fever higher than 101°F (38.3°C)**
- **Inconsolable crying for an extended period**
- **Poor or no appetite**
- **Severe diarrhea**
- **Projectile vomiting**
- **Appears lethargic or floppy**
- **Any other unusual behavior**

Dehydration in infants can be very serious. If your baby exhibits the following warning signs, call the doctor right away:

- **Baby wets fewer than five or six diapers/nappies in a day**
- **Baby's urine is dark yellow or orange (it should be pale yellow)**
- **The soft spot on baby's head is sunken**
- **Baby is listless**
- **Baby has fewer than two loose stools a day**

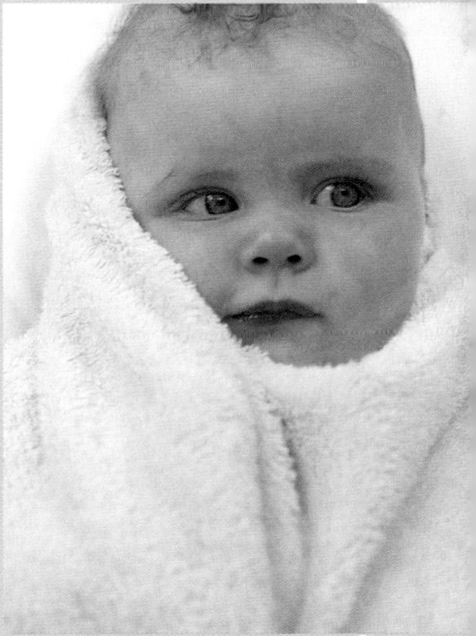

outfitting your car

Your car will need to be equipped with a regulation car seat from the moment you leave the hospital, but there are some other handy items that you might want to keep with you, as well, including some of the following:

Hands-free cell phone
Brief list of emergency numbers for your purse/handbag and glove compartment.
A car travel bag filled with emergency water, extra formula, baby wipes, diapers/ nappies, a blanket, and an extra change of baby clothing. (If you're nursing, an extra shirt for you is a good idea – in case of leaks!)
A rear-view mirror that allows you to see baby in the back seat.
Soothing lullabies or a classical music CD to play for baby *and* you!
A small, mesh laundry-type drawstring bag to store a selection of loose baby toys.
A sunshade – purchase one that you can attach to the window to protect your baby from harsh sunlight.

insurance, guardians, & savings accounts

None of us wants to dwell on the negative, especially not when a new life has just begun and we have a gorgeous new bundle of joy to focus on. But part of being a responsible parent includes taking steps to be prepared for emergencies, and those must include every eventuality. Now that baby has arrived, new parents need to talk about serious subjects such as life insurance and health insurance. It is also important – although rather sobering – to create a last will and testament, and to designate a guardian for your child in the event of catastrophe.

survival checklists

Lists can bring a semblance of order to chaos, and therefore new mothers can only benefit from them! The following lists are intended as helpful examples that might inspire you to create your own.

weekly household shopping list

Dairy – milk, eggs, cheese, yogurts
Soy products
Meat, poultry, fish
Bread, rice, cereals, grains
Dry goods – flour, sugar, salt
Soup, broth
Fresh vegetables
Fresh fruits
Juice
Condiments/spices
Cleaning supplies/laundry supplies

baby needs shopping list

Diapers/nappies
Wipes
Baby wash, lotion, diaper/nappy rash ointment
Formula, bottles, nipples/teats, bottle brush

doctor's visits/baby's records

Date of visit
Developments and milestones
Immunizations
Medications/prescriptions
Instructions

babysitter instruction sheet

Emergency contact numbers (mother's cell phone number, grandparents' home number, etc.)
Details of feeding times
Details of nap and bedtime
Activities (go for walk, feed ducks, etc.)
Special instructions, (heating up food, any allergies, special toys at nap time, etc.)

emergency numbers list

Mother's cell phone/home phone
Pediatrician/GP's surgery
Dad's office and cell phone
Lactation specialist
Gynecologist/midwife
Mother/father (grandparents)
Friend
Insurance

one year graduation certificate

You've done it! You're officially through your first year of motherhood, and you should be proud of yourself. By now you've managed to juggle your numerous responsibilities, schedule endless projects and duties, and you've most probably watched your baby cut his or her first teeth.

The trick to surviving the first year of motherhood is having the willingness to ask for help when you need it. However, as you quickly realized, at the end of the day *you* are the top authority on your own child, and your survival, and that of your infant, has been primarily due to the efforts you put forth. Congratulations!

congratulations!

____

(name)

has successfully mastered the challenges of the first year of motherhood, and is hereby granted all the bragging rights, kudos, respect, and pride that go with such a hard-earned, worthwhile honor!

picture credits

Key: a=above, b=below, r=right, l=left, c=center.

Dan Duchars: **pages 35r, 36l, 48, 48–49, 52, 53a, 59, 62, 63, 64r, 66l, 67r, 68, 69r, 72, 73, 87, 89l, 90, 96–97 main, 98, 101b**

Chris Everard: **pages 79a, 99**

Winfried Heinze: **pages 22 & 23a** (a family home in Holland designed by Jaspar Jansen of i29 design/ www.i29.nl), **23c** the Collettes' home in Holland designed by architect Pascal Grosfeld/www.grosfeld-architecten.nl; **23b, 32r, 37, 40–41** www.i29.nl as before, **42, 50 inset, 67l, 77l**

David Munns: **page 108**

Daniel Pangbourne: **pages 38–39, 76l, 78, 79b, 88, 91, 100**

© Stockbyte **Pages 61a, 77r**

Debi Treloar: **pages 4, 6, 8, 12–13 main, 14–19, 25, 26, 28–29, 32l, 33, 34, 44–45 main, 46, 53b, 54, 56r, 57, 61b, 64l, 65, 66r, 69l, 70–71, 76r, 82, 86, 92–93, 106, 107**

Chris Tubbs: **page 39**

Polly Wreford: **endpapers, pages 1, 2, 3, 5, 7 both, 10, 11, 12l, 20, 21, 24, 27, 30–31, 31, 35l, 36r, 40, 44 inset, 47, 50–51 main, 55, 56l, 58, 60, 74, 75, 80, 81, 82–83, 84–85, 89r, 94, 97, 101a, 102, 104, 105, 109, 110–111**